Staying Well:
Strategies for Corrections Staff

Caterina Spinaris Tudor

emis
Evangelism and Missions
Information Service
www.emisdirect.com

BILLY GRAHAM CENTER
at Wheaton College

Staying Well: Strategies for Corrections Staff
By Caterina Spinaris Tudor

Copyright © 2008. Published by Evangelism and Missions Information Service (EMIS), a division of the Billy Graham Center at Wheaton College.

EMIS
P.O. Box 794
Wheaton, IL 60187
Phone: 630.752.7158
Email: emis@wheaton.edu
Website: www.emisdirect.com

ISBN# 978-1-879089-47-1

CONTENTS

Acknowledgment

The Institute for Prison Ministries (IPM) is grateful to the correctional officers who provide a valuable service to keep our communities safe through offender security and rehabilitation. This booklet is created in partnership with Desert Waters out of our concern for the well-being of correctional officers. Thank you for your service.

Endorsements

"**This book is open and honest about the tough job corrections officers do** everyday and the impact it can have on them and their loved ones. It validates the need to stay physically, emotionally, and spiritually healthy to be effective in this work. Those who can strike a balance in those three areas are truly the best in the business."
—*Belinda Stewart, communications director, Washington State Department of Corrections*

. . .

"The information in this booklet should be shared in every academy and training that occurs in local, state, and federal prisons and jails. It is **accurate, concise, insightful, and comes from years of information gathering.**"
—*T.C. Brown, corrections professional*

. . .

"Correctional workers are the most misunderstood of all law enforcement professionals. This booklet addresses some of the issues faced by correctional professionals and offers techniques and skills to ensure that the correctional worker career is enjoyed and that stresses of the job are mitigated. This is **an excellent resource for anyone working in corrections, their family members, or anyone providing assistance to a correctional professional**. It is written in understandable language and gives real examples of issues faced."

—*Dr. Manuel A. Cordero, former assistant to the Bureau of Prisons' Chief of Chaplains*

Foreword

Dear Correctional Worker,

Stop! Do not discard this booklet. *Put it in your pocket, and read it when you get home. As a fellow officer, I implore you to take a long, hard look at the information contained in the following pages. For too long we have been told that dying eighteen paychecks after retirement is "part of the job." We have been told to "suck it up" when we were down and to ignore our feelings, all to keep the image that we are tough. Do not misunderstand me. I am not the new generation touchy-feely type; however, this booklet contains a wealth of suggestions.*

It is time for correctional officers as a family to begin healing. This healing is emotional, and as this booklet suggests, also part spiritual. We have known too many partners who have taken their own lives or destroyed their own lives through addiction. Honor those men and women by taking the steps necessary to take care of not only yourself, but also your family. No good deeds are more honorable than those carried out every day by our nation's anonymous protectors. Make no mistake: you are one of them.

—Sgt. Barry Evert, a correctional sergeant at California's Pelican Bay StatePrison, has been with the California Department of Corrections and Rehabilitation for eight years. He has been with the California Department of Corrections and Rehabilitation for eight years. His specialty lies in teaching riot tactics and officer safety improvement.

"I Am a Correctional Professional"

Anonymous

I am a PERSON

I am young and old, tall and short, man and woman; and I am of all faiths

I am a father, mother, brother, and sister; I am a son and a daughter, and I am a single parent

I am from all parts of this great country, and I am a citizen of my community

I wear a uniform; I maintain the highest standards, and I represent my agency

I see things that hurt my soul and damage my spirit, but I maintain hope

I lead by example, and I am a good and decent human being

I have a family of loved ones at home and a family of partners at work

I feel, I care, I rejoice, I am a **PERSON**

I am a WORKER

I am well-trained and part of a good team

I work with men, women, and youthful offenders; I work with many cultures, races, and faiths

I work evenings, nights, and weekends, holidays and birthdays

I stand at a post, man a tower, carry a gun; I transport, search, and move offenders

I train staff, write policy, maintain standards, and keep safety high

I supervise good people and hold my partners accountable

I maintain buildings, locks, vehicles, radios, phones, computers, fences, and weapons

I work behind the scenes in cramped offices to make sure the ship keeps running smoothly

I am sometimes verbally and physically abused, yet I maintain my professionalism

I accept that my work is stressful; yet I maintain my honor, I am a **WORKER**

I am a PROVIDER

I provide good food, clean clothes, and protection

I provide education, vocation, work skills, and opportunity

I provide GED, reading, writing, and math classes, and recreation

I provide medical, dental, and vision care; I provide hospice care and dignity

I provide reentry opportunities, legal access, and religious programs; I provide hope

I provide mental health, substance abuse, and anger treatment

I provide a bed, a roof, warmth, and food, I am a **PROVIDER**

I PROTECT

I keep offenders safe while sleeping, working, resting, and playing

I supervise parolees and offenders in community corrections and ISPs

I provide suicide watch to protect people from themselves

I control contraband and maintain facility and public safety

I control access; I keep offenders in and others out

I protect offenders, partners, visitors, and volunteers from harm

I protect the public, 24 hours a day, 365 days a year—all day, every day

I PROTECT Them, Us, and YOU

I do what I do because I serve my community, my agency, my state, and my country.

I am a Person, a Worker, a Provider, and a Protector. **I am not a guard; I am your Correctional Professional.**

CHAPTER ONE

The Toll of the Job

Corrections staff operate in an environment of chronic stress, continual alertness, and the ever-present possibility of violence. Staff are exposed to violence in a multitude of ways, the impact of which adds up over time. They read about crimes in offender files, view videos of assaults or riots for training purposes, hear or read about assaults on the news, witness such assaults firsthand, or they themselves become victims of violence. Gradually, this exposure, coupled with the high stress and need for continual watchfulness, breeds symptoms of distress. As one worker explained, "What I come across at work wounds my soul."

Although there are training and services to assist staff, in the absence of using effective individual and organizational coping strategies, a build-up of negativity can lead to stress-related illnesses, substance abuse, divorce, family violence, and suicide. Not surprisingly, it can also result in high rates of sick leave, disability, and staff turnover. Of course, some individuals will be more susceptible and some more resilient to these pressures than others.

The following stories illustrate some of the struggles faced by staff and are composites of staff stories, with details altered or removed to render them unidentifiable. These are not "problem children." On the contrary, they are hardworking, seasoned, and conscientious employees. When you come across people like them, you would never guess they are struggling. They wear their "I'm good!" mask, acting like nothing bothers them. Are their struggles rare? Unfortunately not.

. . .

"I've been a correctional officer for fifteen years. Lately, I've been short-tempered with my family. Four months ago I was viciously assaulted by two offenders. Since then, I've become very somber. I don't smile much and I keep replaying the incident in my mind. Even when I close my eyes at night, I see the offenders lunging at me. In the morning, I wake up feeling exhausted. Lately, I started drinking before going to bed. It helps me fall asleep. I don't like doing that, but I can't see myself going to a shrink."

. . .

"I've been a correctional officer for nine years. In social situations I get terribly tense. I feel like I'm in danger and that I need to get out or push people away, even though I know there is no danger. I make excuses to avoid social events unless I know that only a handful of people will be there. When I am given a table at a restaurant (or even have to sit in a room with other people), if I can't put my back up against a wall, I get very stressed. I hate not being able to enjoy social situations and feel like life is passing me by."

I've been a correctional healthcare provider for seventeen years. I'm fifty-five years old, twice divorced. Time is ticking. I can't shake the anxiety and depression, even while I am on medication. I had a heart attack five years ago. I have nowhere to turn. I don't want to be a burden on anyone. A week ago I did a practice run on empty with my thirty-eight, but when I loaded it, I could not go through with it. If anyone knew how I'm feeling, I'd be taken to the funny farm in a straightjacket."

. . .

"*I've been a correctional educator for nine years. The job is getting to me. I often catch myself treating my two boys like offenders, screaming at them if they make any noise, and expecting them to do as I say immediately. They don't deserve that kind of treatment. My wife is fed up with me being mad all the time. If she tries to argue with me about anything, I blow up. If the house is messy when I come home, I fly off the handle. I then take it upon myself to clean the entire house until everything is clean and tidy to the extreme. I can't relax until I'm done. I'm ashamed of my behavior and I don't like living like this. I can't go to the doctor for anything related to mental health because if it gets back to work I'll lose respect and perhaps even opportunities for promotion.*"

. . .

"*I've been a correctional employee for thirteen years. I can't seem to get along with anyone anymore. The only people I want to be close to are my husband and my daughter, and they don't want to be close to me because*

I am so miserable all the time. I get to the point where I feel like I just can't stand my job anymore, but then I go back. I complain to my husband nonstop. I sit alone and cry when no one is around. Honestly, I'm nervous about going in these days. We have many gangbangers who (I hate to admit) intimidate me. And we have some staff who make each other's lives hell. Sometimes I don't know who's harder to take—the offenders or the staff. When I really think about it though, it's the staff that is the worst. With offenders, I know what to expect. But with co-workers, I never know what some of them are going to pull."

. . .

"I've been a correctional worker for seven years and am finding it's changing me—and not for the better. I am negative, tired, and gloomy. I know I wasn't like that before starting this profession. I used to enjoy hanging out with and meeting new people. Now I just don't like people anymore. I don't even like myself these days, the person I'm becoming. I can't go on raising a family feeling so grouchy and exhausted. When I applied for the job I was sold—I loved the idea of being a correctional officer. My, was I in for a disappointment!"

. . .

Realities such as these provide the motivation to keep the issue of career survival for correctional staff in the forefront. Staff need both the permission to safely acknowledge their struggles and effective practical tools for dealing with the impact of their jobs. This booklet is about providing you with information to increase your awareness of how your job may be changing you and also ways to deal with those changes.

How Changes Happen

As a result of talking to hundreds of corrections employees over the years, we have observed a pattern of change that stems from the employees adapting over time to the impact of the corrections workplace. This pattern involves the following phases and associated personal change:

"Honeymoon": New recruits are on a "high"; they are excited, motivated, committed, and ready to make a difference. Their self-esteem soars as they start their new career.

Work obsession: Rookies begin to climb a steep learning curve as they encounter the job's situational complexity and interpersonal dynamics with other staff and offenders. Characteristics of this phase include:

1. being consumed by the job, working hard, and wanting to earn co-workers' and supervisors' approval and acceptance;
2. volunteering for just about every team at every opportunity;
3. longing to do something exceptional, even heroic;
4. feeling like they belong to something solid— a family; and
5. having work become their identity

Bubble bursting: After a while, unexpected things begin to happen. These may include the employee:

1. frequently becoming involved in adverse interactions with co-workers or supervisors;
2. feeling personally attacked by other employees;
3. feeling mistreated, betrayed, humiliated, abandoned, scapegoated, and later feeling disappointment, confusion, and bewilderment;
4. feeling as though some of the passion for the profession beginning to evaporate (given that trust is hard to come by in corrections, once it is damaged, it is very difficult to get it back); and
5. feeling ambivalence setting in and no longer feeling that working in corrections is such a great idea.

Despite all this, the employee may keep his or her misgivings to him or herself, put on a brave face, and keep on charging ahead.

Wall building: This phase is represented by:

1. negative experiences continuing to accumulate, and the accompanying emotions remaining undealt with or "stuffed";
2. disillusionment, fear, anger, and resentment mounting and morale sagging;
3. a lack of job engagement or focus;
4. a belief that they are entitled to breaks and exceptions to the rules (they no longer aim to excel and begin cutting corners);
5. errors beginning to occur;
6. failure to accept constructive criticism and reacting negatively to feedback; and
7. distance from co-workers increasing or they

begin hanging out with other disgruntled employees.

Corrections fatigue: This stage is characterized by:

1. cynicism, negativity, and hopelessness; and
2. staff settling for career survival (hanging on until retirement or until they can find another job).

Fatigue or fulfillment: As time passes, staff either sink deeper into corrections fatigue (see next chapter) or become compelled to find solutions to regain their passion for their profession. This requires:

1. learning to process the emotional impact of the job and balancing work with self-renewing activities;
2. building and utilizing an effective support system;
3. developing conflict management and other interpersonal skills; and
4. finding positive meaning in one's work, either through personal growth or through helping offenders or other staff.

If this stage is not negotiated successfully, staff remain stuck in corrections fatigue, with disastrous outcomes to themselves, their families, and their workplace. Sadly, for some this is the end of their professional development in corrections. For others, the realization comes that they would be happier being employed in another line of work.

Riding the waves: Those who discover ways to enjoy corrections fulfillment also find out that even the most skilled staff experience ups and downs. The key at this stage is:

1. accepting that such fluctuations occur to the best in the profession and
2. figuring effective ways to get back on track.

This involves the development of resilience— the capacity to bounce back after disappointments or traumatic experiences. One way to achieve this is remembering to create positive meaning out of negative life situations—learning to find silver linings in every cloud.

CHAPTER TWO

Corrections Fatigue

"Corrections fatigue" is a term I coined to describe the cumulative impact of workplace stress on corrections staff. The concept and its properties are based on the works of Lisa McCann and Laurie Anne Pearlman[1] and Karen Sakvitne and Laurie Anne Pearlman.[2]

Engineers speak of a phenomenon that occurs with metal. A perfectly good piece of metal, when stressed or bent repeatedly, eventually becomes pliable, weaker, and "fatigued." Metal fatigue can happen to even the strongest of stock, and the changes that occur go all the way down to the molecular level. When metal becomes fatigued, even bridges can collapse. In a similar fashion, corrections staff change as they try to accommodate job challenges. The changes can hardly be detected at first. However, they begin to show after a couple of years or so of working in corrections. These changes, due to cumulative and repetitive stresses of correctional work, are what I call "corrections fatigue."

Corrections fatigue amounts to the gradual

---

1. 1990. *Psychological Trauma and the Adult Survivor: Theory, Therapy, and Transformation.* New York: Brunner/Mazel.
2. 1996. *Transforming the Pain: A Workbook on Vicarious Traumatization.* New York: W.W. Norton & Company.

wear-and-tear of the body, soul, and spirit of correctional officers. During a correctional worker's shift, safety and logistical concerns are ever present and of paramount importance. There is little time to deal with the emotional impact of high-intensity workplace events. Thoughts and feelings usually remain unprocessed and unaddressed. Over time, they add up to be a formidable burden. When the impact of work-related stress reaches a critical mass, the telltale cracks of corrections fatigue become evident.

Destructive changes occur in the way officers view themselves, other people, and life in general. Self-defeating patterns set in regarding how to take

The impact of corrections fatigue does not remain confined to staff alone. It eventually "spreads" to loved ones.

care of themselves and how to handle challenges. Anger, anxiety, and pessimism can become the employee's dominant emotional states. Substance abuse and a multitude of other escapist behaviors, such as sexually acting out through multiple partners or pornography, become a way of life for some. High turnover, poor physical and mental health, divorce, and alarming suicide rates are not far behind.

And the impact of corrections fatigue does not remain confined to staff alone. It eventually "spreads" to loved ones, also affecting their worldviews and relationships. Left unaddressed, corrections fatigue wreaks havoc on the professional and personal lives of staff and their loved ones.

Corrections fatigue is a nearly unavoidable occupational hazard. Few employees are immune, and changes usually happen gradually over time. Unless countered, they can become the "default" way staff use to cope both on and off the job. The experience of corrections fatigue is emotionally distressing, as it injects negativity into a person's life. Sounds grim, doesn't it? There is good news, though: corrections fatigue can be dealt with, and even be prevented!

Corrections fatigue is proposed to affect the following areas of a person's self: identity, worldview, spirituality, core beliefs about meeting key needs, self-management, coping behaviors, and interpersonal tactics.

Identity: As a result of corrections fatigue, staff may experience themselves one-dimensionally as super cop (law enforcer), hero, rescuer, victim, or wimp. Thought patterns may include any of the following:

- *"I'm tough, a warrior."*
- *"Nothing gets to me."*
- *"I'm a glorified waiter and a human doormat."*
- *"I'm a coward."*

Worldview: The lens staff view the world, especially people, through is distorted. They may end up experiencing others as dangerous, dishonest, untrustworthy, as "cons," or as "bad." They may dehumanize whoever is seen as different from them.

They conduct relationships in the power terms of winner-loser, conqueror-conquered, predator-prey, abuser-victim, top dog-underdog. Thought patterns may include any of the following:

- *"Watch out or they'll play you."*
- *"They'll try to use you."*
- *"You can't trust anybody."*
- *"They're all worse than animals."*

Spirituality: Over time, staff succumbs to cynicism about life, a sense of separation, distancing from others, and futility in their endeavors. Thought patterns my include any of the following:

- *"No one cares about anything outside of themselves."*
- *"I'm on my own."*
- *"True love and honesty only happen in the movies."*
- *"Kindness is weakness."*

Factors that Contribute to Corrections Fatigue

Below are nineteen factors that may contribute to corrections fatigue.

1. Nature of the job. Corrections work, especially custody, tends to be routine and monotonous, even boring at times. Employees may feel as if they are incarcerated alongside the offenders. When a fight breaks out, however, staff are transformed from glorified (to use the words of a correctional officer) "sitters" and "waiters" to warriors on the frontlines. The intensity of the stress response can be exhausting, even though it may feel exhilarating at the time.

2. Role conflict. Corrections officers are faced with the dilemma of dual roles—custody and rehabilitation. They are expected to confront insubordination and administer consequences to offenders. At the same time, they are supposed to be helpful, de-escalate tensions, and teach offenders how to behave in more socially appropriate ways. These requirements are often experienced as contradictory by staff.

3. Nature of the organization. Like any large bureaucracy, corrections systems tend to be impersonal. Given the paramilitary structure of corrections, it is easy for staff to feel they are regarded by administration as numbers, not persons. The chain of command does not encourage 2-way communication or input from lower ranks to higher ones; this increases the staff's sense of alienation.

4. Staff culture. The corrections work culture, like law enforcement, is one of "machismo," of toughness. It is considered an unacceptable weakness to admit to emotional struggles or to own up to not knowing something or to having made a mistake. When staff, especially security personnel, hear rumors that a colleague is dealing with some emotional baggage and—God forbid!—has even sought professional help for it, they may act like that person is no longer worthy of respect. They may put that person down, make snide comments in his or her presence, or avoid him or her altogether.

5. Socio-cultural and political contexts. Not being respected by the general public as a branch of criminal justice, not having the negative impact of the workplace acknowledged, being stigmatized by association (as people who deal with criminals), and being under-funded all add to the staff's disgruntlement and sense of victimization.

6. Nature of some offenders. Staff are managing increasingly defiant, violent, and/or mentally ill offenders who, naturally, resent their loss of freedom. Offenders begrudge and may attempt to attack their "keepers," the staff. Prisons are intrinsically unsafe places to work in.

7. Negative workplace environment. The prevailing undercurrents of the prison environment are: anger, hate, aggression, and fear, coupled with the scarceness of tenderness and compassion. Lack of natural beauty adds to the oppressive ambiance.

8. Frustrating work situations. Staff get irate when they perceive themselves to be on the receiving end of unfair treatment, bullying, or provocation either by offenders or by other staff. They may get equally upset if they witness what they perceive to be unfair or disrespectful treatment of their co-workers by supervisors or administration.

9. Overload. Understaffing and offender overcrowding do not need further explanation as sources of corrections fatigue. What is needed is greater acknowledgment by administration of the extreme demands placed on staff and appropriate action taken to remedy those as much as possible within the confines of the agency's budget.

10. Exposure to traumatic experiences. Corrections staff witness injuries and death and suffer assaults themselves—from punches to attacks with shanks to body fluids being thrown on them. Exposure to brutality and fatalities leave staff traumatized. Staff often end up experiencing Post-Traumatic Stress Disorder symptoms, which may include: physiological arousal, memory intrusions, emotional numbing, and avoidance. They may also experience symptoms of generalized anxiety, panic disorder, and depression. Given the culture of toughness, these conditions frequently remain undiagnosed and untreated, thus eroding staff's mental health, judgment, and performance.

11. Sexual harassment. Staff may be sexually harassed by co-workers through jokes, comments, or suggestions for sexual involvement. Targeted individuals may be threatened with retaliation if they do not comply with sexual requests. This is an extreme source of distress for employees who are preyed upon by co-workers. Women staff in particular are exposed to sexual harassment by offenders through comments or sexual acting-out behaviors, such as offenders exposing their genitals or masturbating in public. On the flip side, staff falsely accused of sexual harassment may undergo stressful lengthy investigations. As a result, they may be stigmatized as perpetrators, even when cleared by investigators.

12. Witnessing policy violations. Staff may become aware of "bad apples," employees who egregiously violate departmental policies. This is an extremely difficult position to be in, especially for new or low-ranking staff if they are alone in their observations, if they see that the code of silence is in operation, or if they do not have the support of their team.

13. Lack of cultural awareness and sensitivity. Lack of awareness of the significance of offender cultural issues, such as the sacredness of certain items of clothing, books or materials used in religious rituals, or the meaning of certain gestures, leads to misunderstandings, mistakes, and even assaults. This increases the staff's stress and can even result in their getting penalized and getting unpaid leave.

14. Insufficient training. When one considers the complex interpersonal exchanges and life-or-death split-second decisions corrections staff make, a few weeks at the training academy and a few additional hours of annual training are clearly not enough. Training needs to be continual and systematic if staff are to be equipped to cope effectively and professionally.

15. Co-workers' negative behaviors. Some employees act in ways that make those around them miserable. They may brag about themselves, intimidate others, or be deceitful. The end result is a workplace where staff walk on eggshells or butt heads. Even if offender-related stressors were entirely absent, the drain of these negative behaviors renders the work environment toxic.

16. "Head-in-the-sand" coping styles. Problems are exacerbated when people try to avoid distressing emotions or circumstances instead of engaging in effective problem-solving. Common means of avoidance are: addictive behaviors, denial of the existence of problems, and aggression against those perceived to be the source of problems.

17. Past personal history. The more incidents of unhealed abusive or traumatic circumstances employees have in their past, the greater the likelihood that their personal boundaries and coping tools are compromised. Work-related pressures and stressful episodes could readily cause such employees to feel overwhelmed, as buried wounds may get reopened or "hot buttons" pushed. Such past issues may include: witnessing domestic violence while growing up; being physically, sexually, or emotionally abused as a child; being raped or mugged as an adult; or otherwise being a victim of humiliation or crime.

18. Current personal stressors. Staff may be experiencing severe stressors at home, such as: mounting debt, sickness, separation, or divorce. These result in staff arriving at the gate already "running on empty," emotionally depleted, and irritable, even before they start their shifts.

19. Lack of effective support systems. Expecting to be "Supermen" and "Wonder Women," staff tend to keep others at arms' length, denying their need for assistance and rejecting help. This leaves them highly vulnerable to stressors.

So how can you combat corrections fatigue and begin to enjoy more fulfillment on your job while also maintaining a healthy personal and family life? To accomplish these goals you have to wage the "battle of the mind." It is to this battlefield we now focus our attention.

CHAPTER THREE

Taking Your Life Back

In order to combat corrections fatigue and maintain a healthy personal and family life, you need to monitor and change the way you think. In this chapter, you will find suggestions for how to do that.

"Repairing" Your Basics Beliefs

As mentioned earlier, corrections fatigue damages our beliefs about ourselves, other people, and our spirituality. Here are some ways to mend the damage:

Identity

- Remember that you have many sides (e.g., spouse, parent, corrections professional).
- Work on keeping the balance among your various parts. Give them equal time as much as possible.
- Base your self-concept on something more enduring than looks, position, or relationships.
- Thoughts like these should fill your mind:

"I'm much more than my job."

"Corrections is what I do eight hours a day—not who I am."

"I'm not responsible to keep everyone in line."

"It's okay not to be able to fix the world."

"I recognize both my limitations and my strengths, and I keep striving to further my personal growth."

"I like myself. I'm good enough."

"What I do matters. It does make a positive difference."

Worldview

- Keep correcting your distorted beliefs that the world is full of bad people. There are many good, honest, and caring people out there.
- Understand the error of over-generalizing from a few to "everybody."
- Remind yourself that the free world is not identical to the corrections world.
- Work on seeing others' points of view.
- Try to argue against your prejudices, looking for exceptions to your over-generalizations.
- Thoughts like these should fill your mind:

"People are too complex to put into just one category."

"I will try to assess each person individually."

"There ARE good people out there."

"Some people DO get better."

"There is more than one side to every story."

Spirituality

- Seek the Highest Power.
- Adopt positive principles to live by.
- Learn to trust trustworthy people.
- Risk depending upon something bigger than

yourself.

- Enjoy the advantages of being part of something bigger than yourself.
- Adopt a spiritual framework that addresses the presence of evil and has a hopeful outlook.
- Indulge in the joys of giving, loving, and helping.
- Thoughts like these should fill your mind:

> *"I value optimism, kindness, and compassion."*
>
> *"Goodness, love, and truth do win in the end."*
>
> *"I am lovable—worth loving and loved."*
>
> *"I am not in charge of the universe."*
>
> *"I am in awe of the beauty of nature."*

Sue's story: Sue got into corrections after her divorce. She had two teens to raise and promised to help put them through college. At work, Sue strived to remember that offenders were human beings, even though at times they acted like vicious killing machines. She never lost sight of herself as a mother and as a vibrant member of her community. She was passionate about being involved in her children's lives and also in building her support system with other mothers, some corrections staff, and her church group. Sue was a stickler about applying the Golden Rule—"Do unto others as you would have them do unto you." She was also a firm believer that you reap what you sow. Therefore, she treated everyone with respect. She often asked herself, "What if one of my kids messes up and ends up spending a night in jail? How would I want him or her to be treated?" So Sue guarded her heart against hating others and against obsessing on paybacks whenever she was not treated like she would have liked. She applied policies with fairness and learned not to sweat the small stuff. As a result, Sue could sleep peacefully most nights.

More Corrections of Distorted Thinking

It is easy to think irrationally. We do not have to be crazy to do that. All it takes is feeling a little threatened or stressed. Below are five reasoning errors[3] that stressed-out corrections staff can get caught up in.

1. All-or-nothing thinking. This involves seeing things or people as all good or all bad, instead of a mix of positives and negatives. Situations are perceived to be all black or all white, without shades of gray. In reality, things are rarely that simple. The solution? Learn to tolerate that life is pretty much a mixed bag. Good things have their drawbacks, and bad things have a positive side as well.

2. Over-generalizing. This involves reasoning from one to all. Just because one person or situation turns out one way, we may come to expect that others fall into the same category. Again, that does not have to be so. The remedy? Remind yourself that each case needs to be examined individually and judged on its own merit.

3. Magnifying or minimizing. This involves the tendency to exaggerate one aspect of a situa-

---

3. These were first published in Dr. David Burns's 1980 book, *Feeling Good: The New Mood Therapy*. New York: Avon Books.

tion, such as a loss or a failure, or to minimize a success or a compliment. The solution? Put things in context and look at the whole picture—the positives as well as the drawbacks.

4. Personalizing. This involves assuming responsibility in the absence of evidence to support that conclusion: "It was all my fault. I ruined it!" The remedy is found in calming down enough to look at a situation objectively. We need to consider all the factors that contributed to an outcome.

5. Mind-reading. This involves assuming things and believing that we know what goes on in someone else's mind: "She meant to embarrass me." The solution is found in admitting that we simply do not know what other people's motives and thoughts really are.

The ABCs of Self-care

In addition to correcting damaged beliefs, below are some general areas to focus on in "detoxing" from corrections fatigue. Implementing these tools on a regular basis will help you enjoy your life on the outside and be renewed when you get back to work.

1. Awareness and Acknowledgment. Be aware of your thoughts and feelings in an objective, noncritical way. What emotions are you experiencing—anger, sadness, anxiety, worry, fear, joy, shame, affection, love? What triggers anger or fear in you? Follow up your increased awareness with confiding in trusted individuals and seeking help from appropriate sources when needed.

2. Balance

- Pursue a meaningful and love-filled life outside of work.
- Engage in healthy routines for transition from work to home life (down time).
- Keep a balance between work and rest/play/healthy distractions.
- Keep a balance between seriousness and laughter.
- Keep a balance between strictness and compassion.
- Keep a balance between judgment and mercy.
- Make time for rest, self-care, and play.
- Set up a non-destructive transition time from work to home.
- Balance being a "cop" and a "helper."
- Balance avoiding your emotions and dealing with them.
- Balance getting invested in work and being detached.
- Balance work and breaks during work (when possible).
- Balance time spent venting or processing traumatic material and time spent engaging in positive/fun things.
- Balance time dealing with offenders who push your trauma buttons and those who do not (as much as your work situation permits).

3. Connection

- Build and maintain a healthy support system through family, friends, church, and sports teams.
- Share with one or more confidants.
- Listen to others, be it at work or at home.

- Express appreciation for help you receive.
- Seek to help and support others.
- Engage in spiritual activities and practices that are meaningful to you.
- Spend quality and quantity time daily with your loved ones.
- Build and maintain a healthy community-based support system.
- Maintain relationships with co-workers based upon respect and caring.

4. Discipline

- Make time for self-caring and self-nurturing activities.
- Practice finding the positive side to every issue and being hopeful and optimistic that things can get better.
- Practice gratitude and thankfulness.
- Correct negative thought patterns.
- Practice compassion.
- Practice communicating respectfully.
- Challenge and correct beliefs, assumptions, and thinking patterns that become distorted due to the work environment.
- Maintain professional boundaries. Repair any damage to them by reminding yourself of the basics of ethical behavior at work and putting them into practice on a daily basis.

Self-refueling Behaviors

In addition to the above general areas, here are some specific behaviors that will help you de-stress.

- Get enough sleep

- Breathe deeply
- Eat healthy and regular meals
- Engage in physical exercise several times per week
- Enjoy downtime; get away from all reminders of work
- Engage in healthy hobbies and "fun" activities
- Spend playtime with children or pets
- Be part of social support systems
- Spend time in nature/outdoors
- Practice empathy at home
- Smile

Andy's story: Andy can look back and see stages in his development as a correctional officer. The first few years he was consumed by his job. People from his pre-correctional days were left behind, as he could no longer relate to them, nor they to him. He kept seeking adrenaline rushes through special assignments, trainings, and video games. After a few years, however, Andy no longer had the zest for working out or putting in for overtime or special teams. His lack of energy was matched by his weight gain, his chronic bad mood, and his lack of desire to do things he used to enjoy. It was hard work to even talk to his wife and children—unless he was arguing with them about something.

Thankfully, after a few years the light came on for Andy. This happened following a conversation with a man he looked up to who had been around corrections a long time. Andy had to gradually relearn how to have a life outside of work, how to disconnect from the intensity of working, and how to begin to find pleasure in simple activities. Relationships, hobbies, and volunteering started creeping back onto his radar screen as he began to cut back on playing computer games and hanging with work buddies at the bar. Today, Andy considers himself the healthiest he has ever been as a husband, father, Little League coach, and corrections professional.

Andy's story is just one of many that describe how corrections employees are affected by their job and how they figure out ways to get their lives back and stay healthy.

Creating Happiness

What we focus on has a powerful impact on our attitude, mood, and overall well-being. Someone has said, "What you take takes YOU." Whatever we choose to entertain in our minds grows in dominance and influence in our souls. If we choose to stew about things going wrong—magnifying the bad and downplaying the good—we are guaranteeing feelings of unhappiness and misery. If, on the other hand, we choose to identify ways that life is going well or ways to make it better, we cheer up. The battle for the emotional quality of our life is shaped by our outlook, what we pay attention to, and what we say. Two great ways to create happiness include:

1. Learning to find something good in challenging situations. The ability to identify benefits in the midst of apparent losses can replace hopelessness with a positive vision for the future. Folk wisdom has captured this truth in sayings such as:

"Every cloud has a silver lining," "When life gives you lemons, make lemonade," or "Let your stumbling blocks become your stepping stones." We need to discipline our thinking processes to detect openings and opportunities in the face of opposition or apparent defeat. We also need to learn how to find the positive in mistakes, mishaps, and bad experiences.

2. Letting your mind meditate on things of beauty, nobility, purity, innocence, and loveliness. Think back on examples of healthy children or pets playing and laughing. Remind yourself of people you admire for their courage, wisdom, or kindness. Come up with examples of individuals who bounced back after bone-crushing adversity. Saturate your mind with images of places of breathtaking natural beauty. Even better, surround yourself with loving relationships, and make the time to enjoy the majesty of creation. Create love-filled memories through joyful interactions with family and friends. Tell your loved ones what you appreciate about them. You can do the same at work. Catch people—staff or offenders—doing something right and praise them for it. Commend them for their efforts. Encourage them for any progress they make, no matter how small it may seem to you. When your mind slides back to its habitual setting of negativity and fault-finding, train yourself to come up with three good things about the person or situation you just put down. (And that includes yourself, as well!) Do that repeatedly until the default setting of your mind becomes the positive option. Being positive energizes you and those around you.

Meeting Key Needs at Work

In addition to the need for physical safety, there are six psychological/spiritual needs which must be met—more or less—for corrections staff to remain emotionally healthy and to function at optimal levels in the workplace. These are the needs for: emotional safety, trust, power, respect, connection, and meaning.

1. Emotional safety. In emotionally-safe environments we expect to receive support when we seek it. We expect to be encouraged and comforted when we are going through tough times. We expect that colleagues will honor our confiding in them and keep our sharing about personal issues to themselves. We also anticipate being corrected in constructive ways when we make mistakes, and to be given helpful tips to improve our performance. We want to hear: "I don't want you to be wounded by careless or cruel words or actions. Your welfare matters to me."

2. Trust. Closely related to emotional safety is the need for trust in the workplace. Trust is the glue that bonds people together. Trust grows when supervisors and co-workers are consistent and reliable, when they keep promises, and when they act in ways that show they have the staff's best interests at heart. Staff earn trust when, no matter what, they are available to co-workers in an emergency. Trustworthy individuals choose to act honorably and honestly, and stand up for what they know to be right even when it is hard to do so. They do not tolerate exploitation, abuse, or victimization of others. Trustworthy individuals are able to let go of old conflicts and grudges and make genuine attempts to resolve issues with co-workers. These types of people will say, "I want you to experience that you can depend upon me and on our team. Your welfare matters to me."

3. Power. Personal power is about the ability to intentionally impact one's environment through being able to: control oneself, make decisions, initiate behaviors, and give input in situations. The legitimate need for appropriate power is met in work environments where leaders are comfortable with delegating responsibilities and receiving feedback from their subordinates. It is also satisfied where abuses of power (such as harassment) are not tolerated. Truly powerful leaders also model self-

How One Officer Maintains a Positive Work Attitude in a Negative Environment

Inmates are young and old, black, white, Latino. They are sometimes psychotic, sociopathic, or social misfits. They are incarcerated for crimes such as: homicide, sexual assault, or drug use or dealing. Some are very bad people; some have just made bad choices, but are basically good people.

To many of my co-workers, these inmates are all lowly people who do not deserve anything. They believe that their actions led to their own incarceration and so are made to feel less than human. They may be treated with indifference and might

control—the ability to restrain themselves when provoked or under pressure. These leaders will say, "I want you to be able to exercise your abilities in your areas of authority, and to take initiative appropriately."

4. Respect. The need for respect is based upon our belief that we deserve decent and fair treatment. Respect is about exhibiting an unconditional positive regard toward others, valuing them, and demonstrating that we consider them worthy of our esteem. Respect is shown through our language, facial expression, and tone of voice. It is also shown in our actions and the ways we choose to treat people. A respectful person says, "I want you to know you are appreciated and valued."

even be ignored when they ask for something. There is a definite "us vs. them" attitude.

We have authority over them and inmates must comply with the rules of the institution. However, there is a great amount of latitude in how a correctional officer may interact with an inmate.

I have found that a correctional officer can have a direct impact on his or her own work environment. How we interact with others on a daily basis can make a great deal of difference in how stressful our lives will become. Everyone wants to be treated with dignity and respect, regardless of who they are or what their charges may be. Take the time to learn the names of those you are working with. Try to look at them as individuals, without passing judgment. Our job is to make

5. Connection. We are social creatures. We need relationships where we can take our masks off to varying degrees and let others see the true "us." Attachments are vital to our well-being. Given how many hours we spend at work every week, it is important that our need for connection be met appropriately and ethically on the job. Understanding, collaboration, and support are the outcomes of connecting with co-workers within professional boundaries. We want people to say, "I want you to know that you belong, you are included, and you are part of the team."

6. Meaning. In addition to being social beings, we need to know that what we do has significance—that it impacts our world in beneficial

sure that the inmates are safe and secure, that they do not harm themselves or anyone else, and that they are not harmed by others. There is a judicial system that has or will judge them and determine their guilt or innocence. We are not social workers; however, we can make a difference in their lives by how we conduct ourselves.

Take a minute and talk with them when they ask a question. By taking the time to respond to their basic needs or answer a simple question, you show them respect. This does not mean you can't say no; however, when a request is reasonable and falls within our facilities' rules and regulations, there is really no reason not to respond to them. If they see you as more willing to work with them, they are usually far more cooperative

ways and leads to the meeting of worthwhile goals. Corrections staff need to be shown regularly and through examples how their efforts make a lasting, positive difference in others' lives (staff or offenders), and that what they do is important. We want people to say, "I want you to find fulfillment through your work, be all you can be, and make a positive difference."

The above six needs are interrelated. Satisfying one impacts one or more of the rest. And frustrating one interferes with the satisfaction of the remainder. When staff work toward meeting these needs in the workplace, they end up communicating love to one another.

when you make demands or requests of them. If you are not facing confrontation on a daily basis, stress levels will decrease and you will not find yourself taking your anger and frustration home with you each night.

Ours is a dangerous job and we can't let our guard down. But we can reduce stress levels by being less negative and conducting ourselves in a professional manner. Many correctional officers use up far too much energy trying to prove they are in charge and may come across as more confrontational than they need to be. By using the communication skills most of us have learned on the job, we can create a more positive and less stressful work environment.

—Deputy

CHAPTER FOUR

Professional Boundaries
with Offenders

Greg has been eyeing an attractive young woman offender who was recently incarcerated. He knows she is in on drug charges and that she engaged in prostitution to support her habit. Whenever he is around her, he experiences a lust attack. It is not long before he starts thinking of ways he could be alone with her in her cell. He tells himself that he will be fair with her and that he will make her jail stay easier by offering her canteen items for sexual favors.

Mary's husband has been gradually pulling away from her the last few years. When at home, he is either on the Internet, playing computer games, or glued to the television. Whenever she gets home from her job at the prison, they barely exchange a few words. Mary has been feeling terribly lonely and unloved and cannot help but notice that some of the offenders she supervises are especially complimentary and nice to her. She longs for that kind of warmth and closeness in her life. Mary can feel herself being attracted to one of the offenders in particular. He is young, athletic, and handsome. In fact, the other night she dreamt of him in a way that made her heart race like it used to when she was a teenager. She hadn't experienced such an exhilarating feeling in decades! Mary knows she is crossing the line with the offender in her mind, but she tells herself that doing so is harmless because no one knows about it and because she would never act on her fantasies. Sadly, Mary is on the slippery slope of getting romantically involved with an inmate.

Anne, however, is an example of a correctional employee who caught herself in time, got back on track, and learned from the experience. Following her divorce, Anne found herself in a place quite similar to what Mary has been experiencing. When she found herself preoccupied with thoughts of a certain offender, it was like an alarm went off in her

Hardly any corrections employee who signs up for the job anticipates getting sexually or romantically involved with an offender.

head. She knew if she did not do something about her neediness, she'd regret it horribly down the road. So Anne got on the Internet and researched anything she could find on the subject of staff sexual misconduct. She sought the services of a professional counselor to work through the grief of her divorce. She put in a request for a transfer to another facility. She joined a horseback riding group and became involved in teen mentoring. Anne got through her crisis unscathed and continues to do well in her career as a corrections professional.

Hardly any corrections employee who signs up for

the job anticipates getting sexually or romantically involved with an offender. Sometime later, however, things may change. How does that happen?

Staff cross the line when they start entertaining thoughts of gratifying their personal needs through offenders in their care. For some, it is all about lust—seeing offenders as body parts, vehicles for pleasure. For others, it is about being told they are attractive, desirable, or loved. For yet others, it is all about power—the thrill stems from being in control of a person in ways that are rarely possible in the free world.

When unclear if certain behaviors are acceptable to engage in with offenders, staff need to honestly answer this key question: What needs of mine would get met by doing this?

Identifying even one self-gratifying benefit to a behavior should constitute a huge STOP light. Whether something "feels" right is irrelevant. Why is getting romantically or sexually involved with offenders wrong? The reason is that staff wield power over offenders. Offenders' privileges, safety, and ultimately their freedom are in the hands of staff. Even when offenders instigate romantic overtures, staff are responsible to uphold professional boundaries. No offender's "offer" or option should be entertained in one's mind or in actuality—no matter how attractive it may sound at the time. Any such behavior IS wrong and there is no way around that fact.

Additional questions staff should ask themselves when tempted to get involved with offenders are:

- What will happen if I get found out?
- What is a fling worth—my job, family, reputa-

tion, freedom?

- If someone in authority over me was watching me, would I engage in this behavior?
- What would I think if a co-worker told me that he or she was engaging in similar behaviors with an offender?

So how can staff maintain their professionalism in the face of romantic or sexual temptations?

Ethical behavior starts with self-awareness and self-honesty. Staff need to acknowledge to themselves when they start going down the slippery slope with thoughts such as: "She is hot," "I feel good when the person smiles at me," "I'm trying to find ways to be around this offender more," or "I enjoy his or her compliments." When staff members get to this point, they need to go talk with someone they can trust as soon as possible—someone who can also hold them accountable for their actions as corrections professionals. Otherwise, it may only be a matter of time before they will act on the temptation, do damage, and get found out.

Ensuring one has a healthy support system on the outside for meeting personal needs is vital "ethical insurance" for staff so that they will not turn to offenders for comfort or feelings of power. Trusted wise peers can also be of help. Mental health professionals may help staff identify ways to manage temptations until they can regain their ethical resolve. And they can help teach staff how to meet their personal needs appropriately "on the outside," and not bring their personal yearnings to the workplace.

CHAPTER FIVE

Families in Corrections

The following is a typical query I get from spouses of corrections staff:

I wonder what has happened to my husband since he has become a corrections officer. He used to be so easygoing. He'd laugh and joke and didn't complain much. After five years in the system, he's somber and can't find joy in anything. He's also become paranoid. We don't go out together much, but when we do, he insists on sitting with his back against the wall. And he's so negative! He finds fault with everything and everyone and tears me down all the time. I'm tired of walking on eggshells around him, yet I can tell he's miserable and I feel for him. Please help me understand!

Family members are usually in the dark about what corrections work entails and how it may affect others. Educating them on the subject facilitates communication and strengthens the staff member's support system at home.

When Work Starts to Affect Your Family Life

If you are experiencing increasing emotional distance and bickering with your significant other at home, the following illustration might be of help to you and your partner:

You've dragged yourself through another shift. As you crawl into your vehicle, you say to yourself, "I made it another day." As you peel away from the gate, images of hateful looks and violence replay in your mind. You head down the road, screaming inside at offenders and other staff. You wonder if taking a swing at someone or kicking something would help. You know you will be home in thirty minutes. Just the thought of having to deal with one more person makes you tense up even more. You're not looking forward to any "Hi, honey. How're you doing?" chatter. How will you handle it this time?

Once again, you review your options. When you make it out of the prison gate, you want to leave work behind. You wish you could step in the shower and wash yourself clean from the crud of the workday. At home you want to focus on getting on with life. Not too long from now you will have to climb into that uniform again and head back to the gate. You don't want to contaminate your "free" time with thoughts about the ugliness of work. You don't want to upset your partner with your anxieties, frustrations, or fears. You don't even want to put your feelings and thoughts into words. Perhaps a couple of beers would drown them and keep them out of sight.

Trying to forget what you've just been through at work gives you short-term relief, temporary reprieve from the bombardment of work pressures. Not talking about work allows you to engage in normal, free-world activities. Perhaps you can do something with the kids or watch television. Your family can continue their regular routine without worrying about you and your work life.

"What good would it do to talk, anyway?" you wonder to yourself. You want to protect your loved ones, to spare them knowing about the toxic work environment you find yourself in daily. Burdening your partner with your workday's struggles would only cause him or her needless worry. Your partner cannot do anything to fix the situation, anyway.

Besides, you don't want your partner Monday-morning quarterbacking you. You don't want to get beat up by comments like: "You shouldn't have said that," "You're going to get yourself fired, and then what?" "I want to talk to that guy myself," or "This is what you need to do next time!" You have enough criticism at work. You don't need to bring more upon yourself at home. You've already got one boss. So, if you don't talk, you won't get lectured or yelled at again at home—at least not for your work performance.

And even if your partner is understanding and supportive, he or she still has no way of helping you and really doesn't understand the correctional culture and its politics. Also, you don't talk because you don't want rumors flying through the community. There are issues of confidentiality. What happens inside the prison needs to stay inside the prison.

And yet you cannot deny the fact that as a couple you are drifting apart. You can't even remember the last time you had a heart-to-heart talk. There are many empty spaces between the two of you. This scares you whenever you acknowledge it to yourself. Your job is changing you, and your partner is blind as to who you are becoming. To him or her, you are a stranger.

Besides, when you get honest with yourself, you can't

help admitting that you do bring your troubles home. You don't talk about what happens at work; instead, you blow up over unrelated, usually insignificant, "stuff." You complain, pick fights, and order people around. Or you hang out at the bar with your buddies after work, and get home numb and artificially cheerful.

The truth is that there is no simple solution to your dilemma. You need to let your partner into your heart if you are to stay emotionally connected. And you need to do it in ways that do not violate confidentiality and do not send your partner into orbit. You need to be able to receive comfort and give it in return.

A friend in corrections told me about the best way he and his wife dealt with this issue. They attended a couples' Bible study with other correctional officers and their spouses. They listened to other couples and shared their own struggles. In the supportive atmosphere of the group they learned a new language to talk to each other and new ways to comfort one another. They learned to pray together and for one another. They learned how to ask for others' counsel.

This may or may not work for you. What needs to happen, however, no matter how you get there, is to gradually develop a common language about how work impacts you. Here are some suggestions:

1. Educate your partner slowly and patiently. Give him or her this booklet as a way to jumpstart a conversation. Go to Desert Waters (www.desert-waters.com) and download additional articles.

2. Talk about the workplace, focusing on your feelings about situations rather than factual technicalities. Share enough to have meaningful conversations about how you are doing.

3. Ask your partner how he or she is impacted by your sharing. Listen attentively to the answer. Comfort him or her if he or she expresses concern about your welfare.

4. If you come from a faith perspective, pray together about both your work and home environments.

5. After you share with your partner, deliberately choose to focus on the present at home. Laugh, play, and relax together. Do something engaging with the kids.

Below are a few questions spouses and significant others can ask corrections professionals to increase closeness:

- How does your usual day unfold? What are the routine procedures you go through, tasks you have to get done, exchanges you have with other staff and offenders?
- What are you expected to do in an emergency?
- What would constitute an emergency in your workplace?
- What are some of the challenges you face at work?
- What are some of your areas of concern?
- What emotions get stirred up at work?
- How can I help you leave work behind when you get home?
- How would you like me to support you

around work-related issues?

- What do you like about your job?
- What do you feel you do well at work?
- What are some of the disturbing things you deal with at work?
- How can we talk about your work experiences enough so I stay close to you, but not too much so you don't feel like you cannot get away from work when you get home?

It is wise to listen to your partner without trying to fix his or her situation. Validate his or her emotions without necessarily taking sides. Let your partner know it is okay to feel very strongly about certain situations. Seek ways to be supportive and comforting without being too "syrupy." Express your thanks and appreciation to your partner for taking care of you and your family. Pray for your spouse.

Learn to listen respectfully and compassionately to your spouse's apprehensions and concerns for your safety. Don't cut him or her off. Your spouse cares about you and loves you. Hear him or her out and offer reassurance, especially after a disturbance in a prison or another such incident makes the news.

CHAPTER SIX

Psychological Trauma

Why are corrections professionals vulnerable to psychological traumatization? Like other law enforcement personnel, corrections staff are exposed to potentially life-threatening and horrifying situations more than the average citizen. Some of these events would be characterized as critical incidents and some not.[4]

In the course of their careers, correctional staff may be exposed to a variety of traumatic incidents: being assaulted; witnessing the gruesome injury or murder of staff members; being taken hostage, raped, and tortured; or being caught in an offender riot. Additionally, staff may have to cut down offenders who have hanged themselves and perform CPR on lifeless bodies. Staff who rush to a disturbance might come upon the horrific sight of an offender stomped to death or disemboweled by other offenders. Or they may be part of the team overseeing an offender's execution.

Observations in wartime have shown that even the "toughest of the tough" can be affected. Psy-

---

4. In the former case, a Critical Incident Stress Debriefing team may be sent to a facility. In the latter, potentially traumatic events are treated as part of the job. Staff tend to just dust themselves off and act as if they have not been affected by the incident.

chiatrists have come up with a variety of names describing the outcome of exposure to horror, danger, helplessness, and death. Shell shock (World War I), war neurosis (World War II), Post-Traumatic Stress Disorder (Vietnam War), and combat stress reaction (1982 Israeli-Lebanon War) are all labels coined to denote the symptoms observed.

The corrections culture has typically tended to leave the issue of staff traumatization unaddressed. Being "tough" is a requirement for the job and a badge of honor for corrections staff. Corrections staff who have gone through life-threatening expe-

The corrections culture has typically tended to leave the issue of staff traumatization unaddressed. Being "tough" is a requirement for the job.

riences or who have witnessed gore may be treated by colleagues with the unspoken expectation that they should remain unaffected by the ordeal. Yet nothing could be farther from the truth. Corrections staff do get affected. A traumatic event can have a lasting biological, psychological, spiritual, and social impact. Corrections staff are human beings who, like the rest of us, are influenced by the incidents to which they are exposed. Corrections staff, too, go through a complex inner process in their attempts to adapt after their exposure to traumatic stressors.

Diagnosing PTSD

Below is a summary of the symptoms necessary for the diagnosis of Post-Traumatic Stress Disorder (PTSD). These symptoms fall into three major categories: memory intrusions, physiological arousal, and avoidance and emotional numbing.

Memory Disturbances. Memory intrusions involve unintentional remembering of traumatic events—"pop-ups" in the mind, nightmares, and flashbacks. Traumatic events are relived repeatedly in one or more of the following ways, which end up re-traumatizing the survivors:

1. Repeated, disturbing, and unwelcome remembering of the event. You may say things like: "I can't get it out of my mind" or "It pops up on its own whenever it wants to, and I can't turn it off."

2. Recurrent nightmares of the event. You may say things like: "Even my sleep is no longer a refuge, a safe place where I can go to escape these memories."

3. Acting or feeling as if the traumatic event were happening all over again in the present moment (includes illusions, hallucinations, and dissociative flashback episodes). You may say things like: "All of a sudden I was right back in the middle of the fight, reliving it all over again."

4. Intense emotional turmoil when exposed to reminders of the traumatic event. Reminders can be internal—one's own thoughts or feelings—or external—cues in the environment that trigger memories of the traumatic event. You may say things like: "When I smelled those smells again, I thought I'd lose my mind."

5. *Physical reactions on exposure to internal or external cues that remind the survivor of an aspect of the traumatic event.* You may say things like: "When I came across my photos after the assault, my heart began to race, and my whole body was shaking so badly that I almost passed out."

Physiological Arousal. As a result of exposure to traumatizing material, a survivor's sympathetic nervous system, which is involved in the fight-or-flight response, becomes overly active. This is not surprising, as the traumatic memory intrusions make the survivor feel like the danger is ever present. As a result, traumatized survivors may have:

1. Difficulty falling or staying asleep
2. Irritability, outbursts of anger, or aggression
3. Difficulty concentrating
4. Hypervigilance (being excessively on guard, always on the look-out for signs of danger)
5. A strong startle response (jumping up, screaming, or physically attacking someone when touched unexpectedly, when there is a loud sound, or when someone enters the room unexpectedly)

Avoidance and Emotional Numbing. To cope with the flood of unwanted memories, survivors make diligent efforts to avoid whatever cues remind them of the trauma. The following are some ways this plays out:

1. To minimize the impact of triggers in the "outside world," survivors learn to avoid certain conversations, people, places, or things.
2. To gain control over the cues in their internal world (one's own sensations, reactions, thoughts, and emotions), survivors learn to emotionally

"numb out," that is, disconnect themselves from their inner lives, becoming unaware of what they are thinking or feeling.

3. Emotional numbing leads to a generalized shutting down of emotions, especially of positive or loving feelings. It also leads to a sense of detachment and emotional distance from other people.

4. Avoidance results in a reduced desire to engage in activities one used to participate in prior to the traumatic event, leading to additional withdrawal from people, places, and things.

"It's all in the past and I don't want to talk about it!" becomes a standard response survivors give to those who mention the traumatic event. "I can't put into words what's going on with me" is anoth-

Trauma survivors may refuse to talk about the traumatic episode. They might also systematically avoid whatever reminds them of the trauma.

er stock phrase. "I just want to be left alone!" becomes a lifestyle. Avoidance and emotional numbing insulate a person from "triggers" in his or her environment and in his or her own mind. Trauma survivors may refuse to talk about the traumatic episode. They might also systematically avoid whatever reminds them of the trauma. They can even forget important details of the incident. Traumatized people can look emotionally constricted and "flat."

These three clusters of symptoms—memory

disturbances, physiological reactions, and avoidance—seem to go in a cycle. The traumatized person gets triggered when traumatic memories flood his or her awareness, resulting in physiological alarm reactions. The distressing nature of the memories and the attending physiological reactions prompt survivors to try to regain control of themselves through avoidance and numbing. For a PTSD diagnosis, the symptoms must last for more than one month. Also for a diagnosis, the distress caused by the symptoms must result in significant impairment in social, occupational, or other important areas of functioning.

You may have experienced a traumatic episode at work and may still be struggling without professional help. Please consider seeking help from professionals specializing in treating psychological trauma.

Secondary Traumatic Stress

During the course of his 15-year career in corrections, Marv has watched a multitude of videos of riots and incidents of offender-on-offender and offender-on-staff violence. He has also witnessed many such incidents firsthand. He's had to cut several offenders down who had attempted or completed suicide by hanging. Years later, Marv vouches that nothing he sees at work upsets him. He has learned to live in a cocoon of detachment, insulated from outside events and from his emotions. His loved ones at home tell him that he's distant, uncaring, and cold. Once in awhile, however, horrific images visit him in his sleep and cause him to awaken startled, his heart racing.

Shelly has worked as a sex offender therapist in a prison for about five years. She is haunted by gruesome details of sexual exploitation and violence that she keeps hearing during group sessions. Sadistic sexual behavior bothers her the most. Images that get conjured up automatically in her mind while listening to offenders' accounts slink into her awareness while she is sexually intimate with her husband. This distresses her deeply and destroys the moment for her. She worries that her

Rick has always thought of himself as a tough guy. Lately, after writing pre-sentencing reports where the victim was a child, he can't shake the pain he feels.

capacity to enjoy sex has been damaged due to what she listens to all day long. Lately, she's caught herself "going away" during therapy sessions—tuning out details of the offenders' actions and sexual fantasies.

Rick, a probation officer, writes pre-sentencing hearing reports. To do so, he has to read through documents related to crimes committed. Rick has always thought of himself as a tough guy. Lately, after writing pre-sentencing reports where the victim was a child, he can't shake the pain he feels. Rick finds himself wanting to cry, but he won't allow himself to shed a tear. He ends up being irritable and angry. More than once, he's caught himself putting off looking through files. Frequently, on his way home, he buys a 6-pack of beer. He then goes straight to the barn to take care of his horses. Rick stays away from his family's happy chatter as much as he can. He worries about his children's safety and often fantasizes about how he would exact revenge from offenders if they hurt one of his own children. And he gets into arguments with his wife who objects to his repetitive and obsessive coaching of his children to trust no one but immediate family.

These correctional employees exhibit signs of a common occupational hazard—a phenomenon called Secondary Traumatic Stress (STS).

When individuals witness others' fear, helplessness, or horror, when they hear or read about the suffering of living beings, the witnesses can become secondary victims of these tramatic events.

Corrections professionals are affected when they are continually exposed to traumatic material, even if the exposure is through hearsay or about past events. When individuals witness others' fear, helplessness, or horror, when they hear or read about the suffering of living beings, the witnesses can become secondary victims of these traumatic events. That is, they start exhibiting signs that mimic those of post-traumatic stress. Being affected by one's job in that way does not mean that one is not cut out for corrections or that one is "weak." Rather, STS is an almost inescapable occupational hazard which is mediated by the staff's capacity for caring.

Staff suffering from STS may be troubled by details of injury, torture, and death that are stored in their memory and intrude upon the screen of their minds uninvited. Staff may be "revved up" physically, experiencing sleep disturbances, muscle tension, a strong startle response, and irritability. This is usually accompanied by an increased perception of threat in their environment—which psychologists call "hypervigilance." Staff may try to avoid certain thoughts, emotions, people, places, and activities. And staff may react to new traumatic material by being emotionally numb or "shut down."

Unless STS is addressed and efforts are made to counter and prevent it, it takes its toll on the staff's professional functioning and private lives. Staff need to know ways to counter and prevent STS at the organizational, professional, and personal levels. These strategies include:

• acknowledging the effects of exposure to traumatic material by admitting to yourself that it is indeed bothering you;

• processing the emotional impact of exposure to traumatic material by talking about it with significant others, peers, spiritual advisors, or professional counselors; and

• engaging in mind-renewing and caring activities to remind yourself that there are still good people out there and to enjoy love, the great healer of soul wounds.

CHAPTER SEVEN

Substance Abuse

Whenever I offer stress management training, I ask corrections staff questions about their most common coping tools. Staff consistently mention alcohol consumption and absenteeism (calling in sick) as their top coping behaviors. Below we will discuss the former behavior, specifically, the issue of self-medicating through alcohol use.

Alcohol is easy to turn to. It is legal and relatively cheap. It is also part of the "tough guy" image to which corrections staff often adhere. Although alcohol is a depressant of the nervous system, at low concentrations it stimulates areas of the brain that produce pleasure. It thus creates a sense of artificial happiness—fake joy in a bottle. In addition to simulating good feelings, alcohol numbs negative emotions such as anxiety and worry, and helps muscles relax. Alcohol can help an agitated person fall asleep (but not necessarily stay asleep).

However, at higher amounts, alcohol impairs brain function, such as rational thinking—even up to seventy-two hours following heavy use. Alcohol suppresses activity in parts of the brain involved in planning and rational thought. It reduces inhibitions, and increases impulsivity and acting without considering the consequences. And long-term alcohol abuse includes damage to vital organs, such as the liver, brain, and heart.

Given the many adverse consequences of alcohol abuse and the specter of addiction, it is critical that corrections staff choose to develop healthy ways to deal with their stressors. One of the most effective coping tools is regular physical exercise. Another is the consistent processing of intense emotions, such as anger, fear, and grief, through confiding in trusted others, allowing oneself to cry, praying, journaling, or seeking professional counseling.

If you wonder whether you are abusing alcohol, answer the questions below as honestly as you can:

- *Do you call in sick due to suffering from a hang-over?*

- *Is your alcohol consumption causing conflict between you and your significant other at home?*

- *Do you drink to feel comfortable in social settings?*

- *Do you drink to forget about your circumstances?*

- *Do you drink to boost your self-confidence?*

- *Do you have the reputation that you sometimes do embarrassing or violent things when drunk?*

- *Have you ever felt guilt or regret for things you've done while drinking alcohol?*

- *Have you caused yourself or your family financial hardship due to your spending money on activities related to your alcohol consumption?*

- *Do you find yourself drinking with people or in*

places you would normally avoid when sober?

- *Do you put your family in danger while drinking, such as driving them around while drunk or exposing them to unsafe drinking companions?*

- *Have you noticed that your desires and plans for the future have faded since you began to drink more?*

- *Do you crave alcohol at certain times of the day?*

- *After a night of hard drinking, do you wake up wanting a drink the next day?*

- *Do you have difficulty staying asleep after a night of heavy drinking?*

- *Has your competence level at work or your efficiency at home dropped since you started drinking heavily?*

- *Is your alcohol consumption putting your job security in question?*

- *Do you drink by yourself, away from people?*

- *Have you ever had a blackout (loss of memory of events) while drinking?*

- *Has your physician ever treated you for alcohol-related health problems?*

- *Have you ever had to go to a hospital or other treatment facility due to health concerns or problems that stem from your alcohol consumption?*

If you answered YES to any one of the questions, you may be abusing alcohol.

If you answered YES to any two questions,

chances are you are abusing alcohol.

If you answered YES to three or more, you are definitely abusing or depending upon alcohol to cope. Please seek professional help as soon as possible. Your health and even your very life may depend upon it.[5]

---

5. The above questions were modified and adapted from a questionnaire used by Johns Hopkins University Hospital in Baltimore, Maryland.

CHAPTER EIGHT

Correctional Staff Suicide

If You Are Feeling Suicidal

Dear Correctional Worker,

Lately you've been thinking that life is too hard—that holding on is not worth the pain and hassle that often go with it. Your thoughts of "checking out" sometimes comfort you and sometimes scare you. They comfort you because they seem like a friend who offers to assist you in a time of need. But they also scare you because of the unknowns that go with suicide and because of its finality. You're not sure you want to take the road of no return. A part of you just hates giving up.

Every year, about six percent of the U.S. population seriously contemplates killing themselves. Having thoughts of ending your life is not unusual. None of us likes to suffer. We all want solutions for our problems, relief for our pain. When cornered, we all want an "out."

I don't know what your circumstances are, but I gather that recent losses, failures, or disappointments are threatening to take you over the edge. Perhaps your significant other informed you that the relationship is over. Maybe you crossed a line at work and you're about to be exposed or are already under investigation. You might be struggling with the embarrassment of yet another DUI. You may have made disastrous investments that wiped out your family's savings. Perhaps you were diagnosed with a disease which, in your mind at least, strips you of your dignity. Perhaps you inherited a family history of severe depression.

Whatever your situation, negative emotions and thoughts appear overwhelming. Sorrow, shame, self-hate, rage, and fear threaten to suck you down into a black hole. A sense of worthlessness, hopelessness, and powerlessness dominate your existence. You feel exhausted. You fly off the handle or

Infinitely better alternatives to suicide abound. If only you persevere long enough and do your part, life-affirming options will appear.

you can barely stop crying. Your mind screams at you, "Loser! You don't have what it takes! It's over for you!" Thoughts of death come camouflaged as a merciful escape.

You may be feeling a powerful urge to end your misery. Please hear me. If you see yourself in what I described above, go see a medical doctor immediately, even if that means going to the emergency room. We are tied into our body's chemistry. If your car's battery is out of juice, you would recharge that battery. Why try to tough it out where your brain is concerned? If a doctor evaluates you and decides you need medication, please accept that. If side effects are persistently disturbing, ask for another type of pill. Take your medication faithfully, as prescribed. Make that a priority, no matter how you feel.

Now, about your situation. Look for a reputable counselor to talk to about your heartache. When we're that down, our thinking is muddled. We despise ourselves for our failures. We are convinced that there is no forgiveness for what we have done—or that we have no viable options other than suicide. We feel hopeless about anyone ever loving us again or about our ever feeling good again. We feel powerless to do what is required to get our lives back on track. Please trust me that your "seeming" worthlessness, hopelessness, and helplessness are distortions—lies that stem from false assumptions and a chemically-depleted mind. You ARE worth loving. Your worth is based upon your sacred spiritual core. It has nothing to do with what you look like, who wants to be with you, how smart or "successful" you are, or how much money you have in the bank.

Infinitely better alternatives to suicide abound. Resolution can be around the corner. If only you persevere long enough and do your part, life-affirming options will appear. Hold firmly to that hope. You'll watch your sense of powerlessness melt away as you gradually become willing to learn more effective ways to tackle challenges in your life and to quell storms in your emotions. Getting through this crisis will result in the addition of many new and valuable tools in your toolbox.

To overcome the darkness, you also need the fuel

of love. Look for a community that will accept you as unconditionally as humanly possible. For some, this may be a 12-step group, such as Alcoholics Anonymous. For others, it may be a faith community or a divorce recovery group. For still others, it may be trusted friends and family members.

Good can come out of bad. Invaluable lessons can be learned as a result of dealing with suffering. Mistakes can be amended. Forgiveness can be found. Relationships can come knocking on your door. Dignity can be restored. Positive purpose can grace your path once more. Peace can be established in your heart. If you don't believe yet that your life can get better, I invite you to piggyback on my hope for you.

In the meantime, you can either contact us by emailing: youvent@desertwaters.com[6] or by calling: 866-YOU-VENT (866-968-8368) or the National Suicide Prevention Lifeline (800-273-TALK, 800-273-8255). If you know you are at risk of hurting yourself, please call 911 for help or ask a friend to drive you to your nearest hospital emergency room. Your life is absolutely worth saving!

If You Suspect a Co-worker or Loved One May Be Suicidal

Staff, family members, and friends need to be on the lookout for signs of suicidal thinking and

---

6. Desert Waters website (www.desertwaters.com) has instructions for getting an anonymous email address. For extra reassurance that your phone number will be blocked on all Caller ID systems, dial *67 (star 67) prior to the number for the Ventline-*67-1-866-968-8368 or our office—*67-1-719-784-4727.

severe depression in corrections staff. Signs of depression include:

- Tearfulness and crying
- Insomnia or hypersomnia (sleeping too much)
- Difficulty concentrating or remembering
- Excessive fatigue
- Loss of appetite or overeating
- Feelings of hopelessness and helplessness
- Self-hate and self-blame
- Irritability
- Withdrawal
- Loss of interest in people and activities one used to enjoy

Most people considering suicide communicate their intent, usually indirectly. They may drop hints by making statements such as, "Soon I won't have to deal with that anymore," "You won't have to put up with me much longer," or "I've come up with a way to take care of things for good." Questions, uncharacteristic for the person, about life after death and about the eternal consequences of suicide should raise huge red flags. "Wrap-up" statements by a person in crisis, such as "I want you to know you've been a great support to me," could also be veiled communications of suicidal intent.

They may even drop hints to see if people care enough to really listen, pick up on their hidden message, and help them choose life. Therefore, addressing a person directly about the possible suicidal content of his or her communication comes as a relief to the individual. Now he or she no longer needs to grapple with the pain secretly. He or she has evidence that others are "in tune" with him or her and care.

Communication of intent may also be revealed through actions. Giving away prized possessions, setting one's affairs in order, making a will out of the blue, or getting a friend to promise to take in a beloved pet if something happens are examples of "red flag" behaviors. In those situations, do not be afraid to gently, yet directly, ask a person about possible suicidal thinking. Asking someone if he or she is suicidal may bring up painful and intense feelings in him or her, but, in and of itself, the question will not make him or her suicidal. Instead, questioning shows your concern, and that

Asking someone if he or she is suicidal may bring up painful and intense feelings in him or her, but, in and of itself, the question will not make him or her suicidal.

you are comfortable addressing this taboo subject. It also tells the other person that you are not judging him or her, and that you can imagine he or she is in a lot of pain.

For example, picking up on a hint, you may say, "You said that this is too much to take. Has it gotten to the point where you're thinking of suicide?" or "You mentioned that nobody wants you, that you're just a burden to your family. Does it hurt enough that you are contemplating suicide?" If the person says "Yes," do not show alarm and scare him or her off. Most people have had thoughts of suicide at difficult points in their lives. Instead, ask, "Have you thought of a way to kill yourself?" If they reply in the affirmative, ask what their contemplated method of suicide is. Then ask, "Do you have what it would take (the means) to carry this out?" If the reply is "Yes," follow with, "Have you thought of when to commit suicide?" "Where?"

If the person replies "Yes" to more than one question, he or she is at risk for suicidal action. Do not get angry and lay into him or her. That would just make the person regret having been honest with you. Let the person know you cannot even begin to imagine the pain he or she must be in. Here are some next steps:

- Ask the person for reasons to die and for reasons to live.
- Empathize with the person regarding his or her reasons for wanting to die, yet gently state that you believe there are other options that are much better than suicide.
- Ask for reasons to keep on living. If he or she doesn't mention any, say, "Something has kept you alive until now. What might that be?"
- Ask, "When you think about suicide, do you really want to die or do you want the pain to go away?"
- Ask, "What other ways can you think of for the pain to go away other than by killing yourself?"

Do not leave a suicidal person alone under any circumstance. If a person has already acted on his or her suicidal intent (e.g., taken an overdose of pills), or is in imminent danger of doing so, call 911, so he or she can be driven to the emergency room securely. Choose life. Don't keep secrets. Explain to the person that you'd rather he or she be mad at you and alive, than dead.

If a person seems really sad, but not in imminent danger, do not leave the person alone. Get two or three trusted colleagues or relatives to stay with him or her round the clock until the emotional crisis blows over. Steer the person away from alcohol. Do calming activities—such as fishing—with the individual. Do whatever it takes to talk him or her into seeing a mental health clinician or physician. Assist the person in finding a professional helper

Staying well in a challenging environment is not easy and requires self-awareness and reflection.

and in setting up an appointment. Go with him or her to the first session (and subsequent ones), if necessary.

To prevent suicide, department policies must openly mention the stresses of the job, have abundant Employee Assistance Program services for those going through personal struggles, and offer treatment for those exposed to critical incidents at work. Public acknowledgment of the emotional fallout of corrections work—coupled with acceptance of the fact that big, tough people can seek help when it hurts—can go a long way toward preventing the tragic loss of life through staff suicide.

Staying well in a challenging environment is not easy and requires self-awareness and reflection.

Identify destructive thought patterns and behaviors, and take measures to undo them. May you be given the strength you need to continue to take care of yourself and to perform your very significant duties at work. Below is a list of resources that offer safe places of support.

Resources

- Corrections Staff Fellowship, www.csfministries.org
- Desert Waters Correctional Outreach, www.desertwaters.com
- The Corrections Ventline 24/7, www.desertwaters.com/b-ventline.htm
- Phone: 866-YOU-VENT; email: youvent@desertwaters.com

We are also concerned about your spiritual life and invite you to read the final chapter that provides a spiritual solution.

CHAPTER NINE

A Spiritual Solution

As I sat on my balcony overlooking California's Newport Beach, I contemplated my life. At thirty years old, I had experienced career success in both law enforcement and the military. Named the Honor Graduate of the Los Angeles County Sheriff's Academy, I was now a Sergeant with one of the most respected law enforcement agencies in the country, and also a Captain in the U.S. Army Reserve. Yes, I was successful in my career, but I was a failure as a husband and father. I was empty and unfulfilled inside, and somehow I knew there must be more to life.

As the sun set over the Pacific, I recalled my early years as a young Deputy Sheriff when I was consumed with my career. I volunteered for special assignments, made as many arrests as possible, and spent countless hours in court. I sought to be accepted by my peers and went out drinking with them after work, later to develop a dependence on alcohol. In the process of seeking to be "Super-cop," I neglected my wife and children and went through a divorce.

The following day, as I ran along the coast, I passed a church and noticed a young couple coming out. I was drawn to the peace and contentment

I could sense in their countenances—a peace I didn't possess. Somehow I knew the peace I sensed in their lives had something to do with the church they had just left.

I was not raised in a family that went to church or talked about God or faith, but I felt there might be answers to my emptiness inside that building with the cross. I fought the urge to go in, thinking, "Church is for weak people, not Sheriff's Sergeants or Army Captains."

But two weeks later, I went to the morning service and heard a message I had never before understood, but that was to change my life for eternity. What I heard were truths I could understand as a career law enforcement officer, and that are sometimes characterized as The Four Spiritual Laws:

1. God loved me and offered a wonderful plan for my life.

2. But I, and all humanity, was sinful and separated from God. Therefore, I could not know and experience God's love and plan for my life.

3. Jesus Christ was God's only provision for my sin. Through him I could know and experience God's love and plan for my life.

4. I must individually accept Jesus Christ as Savior and Lord; then I could know and experience God's love and plan for my life.

I now understood why career success, possessions, alcohol, or people could not fill my emptiness. The truth of what philosopher Blaise Pascal once said came to mind: "There is a God-shaped vacuum in the heart of every man which cannot be filled by any created thing, but only by God, the

Creator, made known through Jesus." My problem was that I had been seeking fulfillment and peace in my life through everything and everyone but the one person who could give it.

A few days later, with the small bits of understanding and faith I had, I spoke to God and somehow knew he was listening. "God, I'm sorry for my sin. I turn from it right now. I thank you for sending Jesus Christ to die on the cross for my sin. Jesus, I ask you to come into my heart and life right now. Be my Lord, Savior, and friend. Help me to follow you all the days of my life. Thank you for forgiving and receiving me right now. Thank you that my sin

After talking to God in that prayer, I knew my life had changed. It felt as though a huge weight had been taken off my shoulders.

is forgiven and that I am going to heaven. In Jesus' name I pray. Amen."

After talking to God in that prayer, I knew my life had changed. It felt as though a huge weight had been taken off of my shoulders. The peace I had been looking for through my own efforts, God gave me as a free gift through his grace and love for me. Since then, I've learned the truth of Jesus' words in Matthew 6:33: "Seek first the kingdom of God and his righteousness, and all these things shall be added to you." As I put God first in my life, all the other parts of my life began to fall into place with a sense of meaning and purpose. The emptiness I had attempted to fill with alcohol was now filled with his love and peace.

God is gracious, and his forgiving hand has given me another opportunity at marriage with my beautiful wife, Ruth. God is at the center of our lives individually and together. Over the past eighteen years Ruth and I have proven that a marriage in corrections work can not only survive, but thrive. I have found that God's plans for my life are much more rewarding and fulfilling than my own. As I have sought to give God first place in my life, I have become a better husband, father, grandfather, and officer. I now see my law enforcement career with new vision, knowing that God has placed me in this honorable profession for his purpose, to be a positive influence in society for him.

—Mike Raneses, retired parole agent, California
Department of Corrections & Rehabilitation

. . .

God loves you and sees the stresses of your job and the impact it has on you and your loved ones. He longs to have a personal relationship with you. It is my prayer that you will accept his invitation today. I want you to be safe, both now and for eternity! If you have accepted Christ as your Savior and Lord, find someone who can help you grow in your new faith and seek out a church that teaches from the Bible that will nurture and support this new relationship with Christ.

How Can I Live Out My Faith in Corrections?

Followers of Christ who work in corrections have a tremendous opportunity to live out their faith. One officer states:

How you interact with offenders and fellow staff can have a positive impact on their lives. While I cannot express my Christian views to them, I can conduct myself in a Christian manner and hopefully be a role model. I cannot hope to make a difference on everyone in our facility, but if I make a positive difference in just one person's life, I think it is worth the effort.

If you would like to learn more about how to know God, and how to live for him in your life and corrections career, visit the Corrections Staff Fellowship at: www.CSFMinistries.org, email: info@ CSFMinistries.org, or call: 714-573-2921.

Spiritual Weapons

Many of you walk past an offender's cell and can feel the hair sticking up on the back of your neck. This happens when your "sixth sense," your spiritual detector, picks up on the presence of evil. There is no question that some of the offenders you manage at work have committed horrible, revolting crimes and have shown little or no remorse.

So how do you protect yourself from the presence of evil that seems to reside behind the prison walls? I'm sure you've heard various answers to this question. I know of only one that is truly effective: the protective power of the Lord Jesus Christ and his name. This may be controversial to some, but please give it some serious thought. Your life may depend upon it. Scripture tells us that Jesus defeated Satan on the cross; as a result, Jesus has authority over all evil. Followers of Christ are given authority to exercise his power over evil and to order it to cease its activity around you, in Jesus' name. Ask God to put his spiritual armor on you every day as you come to work.

Thank you for the sacrifices and service you provide for society. May you and your loved ones find strength, help, peace, and rest as you trust in the Most High God.

Final Note from the Author

You may wonder what I know about corrections work, especially since I've never worked behind the walls or in any other law enforcement capacity. Well, in many ways, YOU taught me what I know about corrections. I've been working with corrections staff in counseling and in training sessions since 2000. In 2003, I founded the non-profit Desert Waters Correctional Outreach (www.desertwaters.com), with the mission to increase the occupational, personal, and family well-being of staff of all disciplines within the corrections profession. Your safety and sanity matter greatly to me!

Thank you for choosing to serve the general public, your state, and your nation by working in corrections. Very few people on the outside comprehend the challenges and dangers of your workplace. Even fewer appreciate the skill it takes to do your very complex and demanding job. As corrections professionals, you must problem-solve on your feet, use people skills and leadership tools to de-escalate conflict at a moment's notice, and exercise self-control in the face of provocation and chaos.

You may choose to share this booklet with your loved ones. I am aware that in many cases your significant others know very little about what you deal with at work. They may watch you change over time, but may not know what to attribute the changes to or how to be of assistance to you. Consequently, they cannot relate well to you when you return home after your shift. I hope this booklet will help your significant others increase their understanding and appreciation of you. I also hope this booklet will give them tips as to how to be of help to you. I welcome you to share your stories or thoughts about this booklet by emailing me at: caterina@desertwaters.com.

Questionnaire[7] to Determine if You Have Signs of Corrections Fatigue

The items that follow can help you identify general areas and specific issues in your life where you may be affected to a smaller or larger degree by corrections fatigue. The purpose of this questionnaire is to increase awareness, not to self-diagnose. Corrections fatigue is not a clinical diagnosis. It is merely a descriptive term that describes the long-term impact of working in corrections.

Desert Waters

Correctional Outreach

a non-profit organization for the well-being of correctional staff and their families

431 E. Main St., P.O. Box 355, Florence, CO 81226
(719) 784-4727 • desertwaters@desertwaters.com
www.desertwaters.com

PHYSICAL			
	Never	Sometimes	Often
1. In a fight-or-flight mode			
2. Low physical energy			
3. Strong startle response			
4. Sleep disturbances			
5. Raised blood pressure			
6. Muscle tension			
7. Headaches			

PSYCHOLOGICAL/SPIRITUAL			
Identity	Never	Sometimes	Often
1. Seeing self as a law enforcer			
2. Seeing self as a victim			
3. Seeing self as a coward			
4. Seeing self as a position, not a person			
5. Losing pride in one's work			
6. Abandoning professional aspirations			
7. Seeing own profession as inferior to other disciplines			
Worldview	Never	Sometimes	Often
1. Believing the worst about people			
2. Dehumanizing inmates/ offenders			
3. Not trusting people			
4. Expecting a game or a lie in relationships			

5. Dismissing people's expressions of caring			
Spirituality	Never	Sometimes	Often
1. Pessimism—focusing on the negative			
2. Sense of futility—"Why bother?"			
3. Loss of trust in a "Higher Power"			
4. Sense of being alone, alienated, and/or disconnected			
5. Cynicism—reduced ability to enjoy goodness, purity, beauty, and/or innocence			
6. Confusion of kindness with weakness			
7. Expectation that evil/the "bad" guys win			
8. Consideration of honesty as a liability			
9. Consideration of love as fiction or a liability			
10. Reduction in capacity for empathy and compassion			
11. Loss of sense of the value of life			
Core Beliefs	Never	Sometimes	Often
1. "I have to fight for everything I need."			
2. "I should forget about trying to get my needs met."			
3. "I can never relax or let my guard down."			
4. "I can't trust anyone."			

5. "People are basically evil."			
6. "I have to get them before they get me."			
7. "I must always stay in control."			
8. "I must win at any cost."			
9. "I'm just a number, a warm body to my department."			
10. "The one who shouts the loudest, wins."			
11. "Nothing gets better."			
12. "Everybody just wants to use me."			
13. "Nobody really cares."			
14. "If I don't get close, I won't get hurt."			
15. "No one deserves respect."			
16. "What I do makes no difference."			
17. "I'm wasting my life."			
Emotional Self-management	Never	Sometimes	Often
1. Difficulty regulating emotions			
2. "Short fuse"—irritability			
3. Anger outbursts			
4. Acting out when distressed			
5. Anxiety			
6. Panic attacks			
7. Emotional flatness			
8. Depression—the "blues"			

COPING AND PROBLEM-SOLVING BEHAVIORS

At work	Never	Sometimes	Often
1. Escaping thoughts and feelings through overwork			
2. Daydreaming about taking revenge on someone			
3. Keeping a low profile			
4. Adopting offenders' values and *modus operandi*			
5. Taking law into own hands			
At home	Never	Sometimes	Often
1. Habitually scanning the environment for danger; hypervigilance			
2. Preparing for "worst case" scenarios			
3. Pursuing instant relief— "quick fixes"			
4. Taking action impulsively due to anxiety, frustration, or lack of patience			
5. Daydreaming about being on vacation			
6. Daydreaming about quitting the job			
7. Using or abusing substances, including prescription drugs and alcohol			
8. Abusing food			
9. Escaping through other addictions (sex, gambling, etc.)			
10. Thinking about or attempting suicide			

Professional Functioning	Never	Sometimes	Often
1. Negative attitude (critical, pessimistic, blaming)			
2. Decreased quality and quantity of work			
3. Low motivation due to apathy and/or low energy			
4. Poor communication			
5. Irresponsibility			
6. Irritability			
7. Obsession about controlling both offenders and co-workers			
8. Worry, anxiety, catastrophizing			
9. Emotion-based/irrational reasoning			
10. Perfectionistic standards			
11. Self-sacrifice			
12. Absenteeism			
INTERPERSONAL TACTICS			
At work	Never	Sometimes	Often
1. "Thin skin"—taking things too personally			
2. Readiness to initiate conflict			
3. Impatience			
4. Posturing, acting tough, showing off			
5. Intimidation tactics, bullying, verbal threats			
6. Physical aggression			

At home	Never	Sometimes	Often
1. "Iron fist" rule			
2. Treatment of loved ones as if they are offenders			
3. Demands of instant obedience & cooperation			
4. Intolerance of others' requests			
5. Intolerance of noise			
6. Intolerance of messiness			
7. In role of the one who keeps everything and everyone under control			
8. Emotional distance & indifference toward loved ones			
9. Withdrawal/Isolation/Secrecy			
10. Abuse of loved ones— verbally, emotionally, physically			
Primary Traumatic Symptoms	Never	Sometimes	Often
1. Getting very distressed when reminded of traumatic event(s)			
2. Reliving the event in one's mind			
3. Recurrent nightmares regarding event(s)			
4. Expecting that one will die early/soon			
5. Expecting not to have a normal life (e.g., family, career)			

6. "Adrenaline dumps" upon exposure to internal event reminders (thoughts) or external event reminders (people, places things)			
7. Inability to recall important aspects of traumatic event(s)			
8. Avoidance of trauma reminders			
9. Emotional numbing, "flat" effect			
10. Trying not to think of trauma reminders			
11. Dissociating, "going away" in one's mind			